I'VE GROWN ACCUSTOMED TO MY FAT

Poems About People, Places and Puzzles

T.C. HOOD

Gotham Books

30 N Gould St.
Ste. 20820, Sheridan, WY 82801
https://gothambooksinc.com/

Phone: 1 (307) 464-7800

© 2024 *T.C. Hood*. All rights reserved.

No part of this book may be reproduced, stored in a retrieval system, or transmitted by any means without the written permission of the author.

Published by Gotham Books (March 5, 2024)

ISBN: 979-8-88775-732-2 (H)
ISBN: 979-8-88775-730-8 (P)
ISBN: 979-8-88775-731-5 (E)

Because of the dynamic nature of the Internet, any web addresses or links contained in this book may have changed since publication and may no longer be valid.

The views expressed in this work are solely those of the author and do not necessarily reflect the views of the publisher, and the publisher hereby disclaims any responsibility for them.

CONTENTS

VERSE ONE: 1
VERSE TWO: 2
VERSE THREE: 3
VERSE FOUR: 4
VERSE FIVE: 5

SECTION ONE

MISS HAZEL 6
FRIENDSHIP 8
CARING 9
FOR DWIGHT 10
THE DIFFERENCE 11
IN AS MUCH 13
BOUND FOR GLORY 15
LIFE AND DEATH ARE FULL OF MYSTERY 16
I AM 18
WHAT SHALL WE SAY? 19
THE LOGIC OF LOVE 20

SECTION TWO

SIGNS 21
THE SNOW TREE 22
REDBUD TREE 23
THE SINGING FOREST 24
FORGOTTEN FLOWERS OF THE FIELD 26
BLAZE 27

MOON MIRROR	29
THE TANGLED WEB	30
A VIEW FROM THE CHOIR	31
GRAFFITI	33

SECTION THREE

FADING TO BLANK	34
A BUSHEL OF APPLES	37
STRAWBERRY PICKING	39
THE NEUTRON BOMB	41
THE BLINDFOLD	43
TERMITES	45
STRUGGLE	47
I AM AMERICA WEEPING	48
CALOUSED CONSCIENCES	50
YOUNG AT HEART	53
ANGEL TONGUES	55
THE LAST WORD	57

VERSE ONE:

Co-Authored:

MARY LOIS HOOD KETCHERSID

I've grown accustomed to my fat

It almost makes the day begin

I've grown accustomed to the meals

I eat each night and noon

Potatoes and eggs, bread pudding and steaks

They're second nature to me now

Like chewing up and swallowing down

I was once serenely skinny

And content with cottage cheese

Now I'm fat and happy

Just eating what I please

I've grown accustomed to the tremor

When I walk into a room

Accustomed to my fat.

VERSE TWO:

I've grown accustomed to my fat.

I like its jiggle when I walk.

I've grown accustomed to the stares.

When I walk down the street

The comments, the jeers,

the laughter, the tears

I'm well adapted to them now.

Like the shouting out, "Hey you!"

I was once somewhat embarrassed.

And would run away and hide.

Now I face them bravely in my size eighty-fives.

I've grown accustomed to the roar.

Of laughter behind my back

Accustomed to my fat.

VERSE THREE:

I've grown accustomed to my fat.

Why should I bother to reduce?

I've grown accustomed to the rolls.

that ooze over my belt

My jowls, my hips, my fifteen double chins

Are so familiar to me now.

They are my massive every day.

They fill each mirror fully,

As I am strolling by

If I again were thinner

I would not recognize "I."

I've grown accustomed to the clunk!

When I step upon the scales.

Accustomed to my fat.

VERSE FOUR:

I've grown accustomed to my fat.
Its second-nature as they say.
I've grown accustomed to the roll.
That magnifies my waist.
The fuss tailors make.
When my measurements they take
Are very common to me now
Like struggling out and struggling in
I was once so slim and supple
My clothes were the right kind.
Now my fat hangs in folds in front
And pleats in my behind.
I'm just a mobile tent
As I go down the street
Looking for my feet.

VERSE FIVE:

I've grown accustomed to my fat

I huff and puff, when I climb stairs

I've grown accustomed to the state of being short of breath

The throbbing, the pain,

it's all just the same.

I'm well accustomed to them now

And doctors' warnings not aside

I take them all so bravely

Even though my stomach shakes

My blood pressure goes sky high.

While my colon quakes

I've grown accustomed to prescriptions,

diets, even threats.

Accustomed to my fat.

Finale

I've grown accustomed to my fat

So please don't ask me to reduce

It's really something special

to be as big as me

For even in a crowd of people

I am all you see

I've grown accustomed to the need

For larger bottomed chairs

Accustomed to my Fat.

MISS HAZEL
[SECTION ONE : PEOPLE]

That's how she was known at the church.

I visited her in her home, but that isn't how I met her.
I met Miss Hazel first, through the eyes of a little girl.
It was our first Sunday visiting a new church.
Our former congregation had simply decided to disband!
After failing to achieve its suburban and intellectual
potential for fellowship,
Members were each choosing different ways to go.
They were finding their way to other congregations
in the city.
We found our way to Vestal United Methodist and
Miss Hazel.
Like many other Sunday School Teachers, Miss Hazel
loved every new child.
Miss Hazel showed that love with flowers from those
she grew in her yard.
Particularly on that first Sunday,
I can see in my memory's eye a small bouquet.
Perhaps five or six stems of flowers
(Was there a wet paper towel around them to keep
them moist?) clutched in one hand of our four-year-old
daughter, Heather.
The smile on her lips and in her eyes told of the
happiness and acceptance she had received that morning.
We learned later that this happened often as
Miss Hazel brought flowers from her garden to the

students in her classes.

I grew up in the Methodist Church.

My Sunday School Teachers had given me many things, including a lasting foundation -— both emotional and rational —in the faith. But no Sunday School Teacher had ever given me flowers.

But Miss Hazel gave this first-time visitor to her class a handful of love in color and scent—flowers.

Miss Hazel taught Sunday School at Vestal for over forty years, until she could no longer do it due to declining vigor and advancing age.

Miss Hazel will live on beyond her ninety-one years on this earth —in her many small acts of kindness that inspired faith in children.

The children and their parents remember and are glad for her witness to the joy of life with God.

Let us celebrate the goodness of Miss Hazel Doyle Endsley's life.

FRIENDSHIP
[SECTION ONE : PEOPLE]

I love you, not only for what you are, but for what
I am when I am with you.
I love you, not only for what you have made of
yourself, but for what you are making of me.
I love you for the part of me you bring out.
I love you for putting your hand into my heaped up
heart and passing over all the frivolous and weak
things you cannot help seeing there, and drawing
out into the light all the beautiful and radiant things
that no one else has looked quite deep enough to find.
I love you for ignoring the possibilities of the fool
in me, and for laying firm hold of the possibilities
of good in me.

I love you because you are helping me to make of
the lumberof my life--not a tavern --but a temple
for God; and of the words of my every day--not
reproach--but a song to Him.

I love you because you have done more than any
creed could have done to make me happy.
You have done it without a touch, without a sign—
you have done it by just being yourself.

After all, perhaps this is what being a
real friend really means.

CARING
[SECTION ONE : PEOPLE]

The lightest brush of lip with lip
The softest touch of fingertips
The whispered songs we often share
These are the signs you care.

The children's portraits on the wall
The desk set cracked once from a fall
The well-thumbed Bibles we consume
Tell of our ways of love.
Chipped wedding plates of thirty years
Teenagers grown up through world-wide fears
Ceramic wish box, books, dulcimers
These things furnish our home.
What memories will make us old?
Will we re-live the tales we've told?
No! Each day brings some new, strange road
That brings us close to God.
Wet snow, blue grass, salt sweat, gray bees
Songbirds, orange skies, chapped skin, oak trees
Lives grown entwined like ivy leaves
Environments we share.

Dare still to care
With each new day
Until we both shall Pass away.

FOR DWIGHT
[SECTION ONE : PEOPLE]

In knoxville a man named dwight
looked around for the very best light "luminescence,"
said he, "provides just the right key to portray.

A young nude in my sight."
For many years past,
Dwight's workplace task was
Framing life's struggles in words.
But as words grew stale
His brush strokes grew bold
Now pictures capture
Young beauties untold.

Birthdays rolled on by!
While songs filled our hearts,
the music played on in our souls.
Paintings expressed
Where words failed to tell…
Gestures and color made whole.

We taste, hear and smell.
see. Find dialogue,
sketches or phrase
fulfillment in life comes to each one.
as friends share the feelings of grace.

THE DIFFERENCE
[SECTION ONE : PEOPLE]

Clothes make the man!
What makes a woman?
Language, the cosmetologist?
Some designing man?

These words cannot explain failures of men
to understand women.
or errors of women who try to understand men.
Does woman make man?
Of course!

We understand the womb that woman carries
the dark and hidden place where bodies grow
at least until that moment of anguished separation
called birth
When what was once part of me

Becomes another.
I am a man.
My contribution was out of pleasure. I gave
the sperm gladly.
I enjoyed the moment.
I did not carry with me
the growing sense of other.
I did not feel my breasts swell with milk for life.
I did not grow weary of the water cushioning a flesh
becoming not my own.

I did not strain through hours of labor to hear that glorious first cry.

Perhaps the difference is:
Women suffer pain to bring new life
While men just pleasure in love
and wonder what suffering is about...

IN AS MUCH...
[SECTION ONE : PEOPLE]

Where does God live?
The thoughtful person asked.
Caught in a time when past assurances
Remained silent...
It seemed that God was dead!

Losses, daily troubles
Surrounded this question, which seemed
More like a desperate cry,
Seeking to restore
The hope that once
Shown forth so easily in the minutia of life.

Does God live at all?

Even the bright sunlight,
The comfort of friends
Could not silence
The ever-present doubt...
Choking the life out
Of the faith that once lived there.
Words became hollow reminders
Of the absence of belief.

How could people be so unkind?

If God exists,

But war and want continue,
How can God be?
Amidst such persistent inequality----
Such nastiness?

Exiled from God's presence
I cannot love to sing
The songs of Joy, of Hope Of eternal Love.

Where does God exist?

God exists in moments of shared concern.
Of reaching across the vast gulf
That separates each soul.

Recognize that in the fleeting moment
When one soul touches another
The mystery
That is God Exists for eternity.

Not in life as we know it
But in life as we are known
In life as we have been known
In life as we shall be known.

God exists in those eternal moments
And God remembers
Even when we forget
Those moments when Soul touches Soul.

BOUND FOR GLORY
[SECTION ONE : PEOPLE]

Woody Guthrie was my kind of man. He was a minstrel.
I'd be like that too.
Jesus Christ was my kind of man. He was a teacher.
I'd be like that too.
Mark Twain was my kind of man. He saw "through" people.
I'd see through them too.
Martin Luther was my kind of man. He was stubborn.
I'd be stubborn too.
M. Gandhi was my kind of man. He loved peace.
I'd show that love too.

Oh! I'll sing you a song
And I'll sing it again
About people who knew
The where and the when
The how and the why
But before I go on …
Remember that you've got
To write your own song.

To sing each day
Until you die
And then you'll sing it
Somewhere in the sky
Or whereever your road to glory goes on

Past people and places
Each singing their song.

LIFE AND DEATH ARE FULL OF MYSTERY
[SECTION ONE : PEOPLE]

God created man.
So, man created God to understand the why of life.

But man still failed to understand how to live, And…
since God was conceived to be more knowledgeable,
and powerful than man.

God needed to become man.
To show man how to live.

Why not? The very idea seems improbable but then…
Intelligent life seems rather improbable, in the
overall scheme of "things" –
That are!!

But if God becomes man such an event threatens
The far off and above all image of a creator.

God becomes too approachable.

Therefore ,
God as man must die in order to keep a believable
idea of God.

Of course, if God dies then God is not an example

of infinite life.

Unless....
The God become Man rises from the dead.

That makes God--God again.
So how is man supposed to live?
Man is supposed to exemplify the love that God
as man exemplified!

"Greater love hath no man than this
that a man lays down his life for a friend."

If you can die for a friend, you know how to live???

Life and Death are full of mystery!!!

I AM
[SECTION ONE : PEOPLE]

A momentary glimpse of truth

Lies hidden in the dark of an unconscious,
not willing to be found corner of Each of us
So
WHAT ENTITLES Another
to lead blindly groping, stumbling in
on a lot of old, lost memories of
things forgotten usefully, perhaps ---
-to stir us to recognize ourselves for what
we are REALLY NOW;

Don't you think Dr. Jones?
master of Free associating,
free will, freewheeling interdenominational
unaffiliated objective scientific advice …

that INSIGHT into self lies in voluntarily
impudently
making the realization
leap-of-faith
assertion,

"I AM what I am !"

WHAT SHALL WE SAY?
[SECTION ONE : PEOPLE]

What shall we say when we grow old,
And no one remembers the victories of youth,
When no one remembers the times we spoke truth?
What shall we say then?

What shall we say when we grow weak
And no one remembers the strength of our hands,
When our clenched fist could turn rocks into sand?
What shall we say then?
What shall we say when vision fades
And no one remembers the eyes that could see
Orange leaves, blue-sky water, and wrens flying free?
What shall we say then?

What shall we say when we grow ill
And no one remembers the bed-ridden man
Dependent on nurses for food and bedpan?
What shall we say then?
What shall we say when we can't speak?
Words will not form; thoughts merely pass.
Mind withers slowly beyond others grasp.
What shall we say then?

We shall say then that God endures!
Faith sustains hope and love will prevail!
Light streams through the curtain shielding death's vale!
We shall pray then!

THE LOGIC OF LOVE
[SECTION ONE : PEOPLE]

The people whom words cannot contain
Force arguments about their acts
Which seem both elegantly good and
Damnably arrogant, perhaps absurd, or intentionally evil .

Too often, knowing motives is confused with knowing men.

And men for all seasons often have mixed motives,
which baffle simpler minds
to whom choices seem so easy—
like black—white, day—night, right—wrong, true—false,
other ways without a middle or a "sometimes."

I often wish I didn't see the merit in another person's view.

Could stand firm with unquestioning mind,
Could be prejudiced and blind,
but then I think, NO.
It's better to say "maybe" and not be so sure
 For a while any way to love my enemy…
 To see his path plainly to understand them.

It doesn't make sense..
Even to me, always
But such is the logic of love

SIGNS
[SECTION TWO : PLACES]

COLD BEEEE R OPEN said the litany on a sign >--------------

HERE.

Pointers

grab

my socketed eyes,

Wrenching my attention from the hammerlock of mind.

Why?

When it's dark, fluorescent night–

Late, walking the street--

Are signs so many;

people so few??

THE SNOW TREE
[SECTION TWO : PLACES]

The snow tree rests silently in the morning mist,
Swaying its feathered branches
carelessly on the wasting wind.

The storm has been here.
Bending each pine's reach
toward the source of storms.

Now the forest waits
Like a huge flock of brood hens
protecting with their wings
the roots of life to come.

REDBUD TREE
[SECTION TWO : PLACES]

Redbud blossoms soft,
Pink clusters on ebony limbs.

You, simple scraggy tree
Gnarled and bent, I know you
by the spring wind
blowing your pink confetti through my garden.

Companion of the dogwood, You glow
indecent in your bare indecency and warm
spring sunlight.
In summer I almost missed you!
Modestly cloaked in forest green
your seed pods dangling
like some overgrown, unkempt shrub.

But last December, I saw you huddled on the
hillside, bent over our still-green holly as if to
warm your cold gray branches in its life.

Now blossoms burst from warmth cluster to
proclaim your glory quietly..
Spring captures me again,
with sudden beauty.

THE SINGING FOREST
[SECTION TWO : PLACES]

Each trunk and leaf whispers to me.
My spirit's fingers trace the giggling leaves.
My tears form little rivers through bark canyons.

My eyes blink.
Walking through the slanting shafts of sunlight
 descending through the dark canopy high above me.

Walking through the forest,
my mind wanders backward to the beginnings.
 Seeds of mighty giants are reborn.
Stumps like blackened stubble
rot scattered among thin new trees.

I could and did get lost in forests
As a child wandering in my grandfather's woodlot.

The forest floor was green with May apples,
Dutchmen's Britches, Bloodroot, Jack in the Pulpit
other nameless wildflowers....

Gardens are so civilized!

Gravel paths and bedded plantings
Pink petunias and purple and yellow pansies
Oh! Gardens are the handiwork of gardeners!
The forest is the jungle—still untamed.

The tangle of the undergrowth provides
a challenge, a path to clear
or just to find.
Small furry creatures blur by me.
The birds perched high above me
call to each other.

The forest and I sing softly to ourselves...
Regardless of the season,
we are one!

FORGOTTEN FLOWERS OF THE FIELD
[SECTION TWO : PLACES]

Lest you should think with too much pride
about achievements strong and brave;
Your name called "Great" now...far and wide
Shall be forgotten in the grave.

Yet memories of lively days
will replay in the minds of those,
who carry on in work and play,
The fragrant beauty of the rose.

Flowers flourish in the field;
Grass grows green and trees stand firm.
Flesh and blood will always yield
unless sustained by love returned.

God's steadfast love, does all inspire.
An outpouring of mercy, grace.
"Forgiveness!" sings the angel choir,
Salvation for the human race.

BLAZE
[SECTION TWO : PLACES]

See the fire.

Triangle of multicolored light
Leap through the cracks
Bending around each log
Flying above the mottled, blinking glow,
In the skeleton of the grate. Shimmering vapors turn to smoke.

Hear the fire.

A warm crackling song,
Above softly falling drifts of gray ashes
The fire hisses and pops
As simmering, steam removes dampness
Still lingering in the rain-wet wood.

Feel the fire.

The red-orange tongues,
Licking the bone cold seeps through muscle
The heat caresses skin
Like some forgotten stray, who in a thoughtful moment
Warmed your hand with its tongue.

Taste the fire.

Swallowing the smoke,

Whose flavor recalls ham and cheddar cheese,
Hot dogs or burnt marshmallows toasted on a stick,
Last summer over a grate-less campfire.

Memories reside in the gods' gift to humankind.

MOON MIRROR
[SECTION TWO : PLACES]

The moon is the sun's looking glass
against the black of space.
We see reflected back and down
men's memories of days past.

But when there's snow, the light
Reflected back and up
Becomes the moon's reflection of the sun.

On earth—or whose or what? Or where?

Where is light possessed – caught and held
Except within the eye of man or beast
Or in the bloom of flowers?

And yet, Each of us may be mirrors
For light passing through
Between life and life.

You or I may be caught in glancing smiles
Until one single beam may gather; fire out

Pulsating in infinite regress
Light penetrates the furthest dim recess

Of our universe.

THE TANGLED WEB
[SECTION TWO : PLACES]

No spider's web that I have seen
hangs tangled—drifting in a breeze
Unless some human hand
has torn its symmetry into strands.

Humans weave the tangled webs
made from half-truths and lies,
Flattering some, while pleasing none,
making and breaking ties.
Friendships endure beyond the bonds
contracts create with words.
The healing touch of sisterhood
transcends life's milling herds.
From cattle calls for extras, to noisy union halls,
We see what our professions,
allow when gathered with our pals.

Day in, day out
words echo on 'til reaching printer's web,
Dispute, conjecture, wit and poem
in ink our voices ebb.

So quickly and so quietly
these tangled webs decay.
The pages burn with captured fire
words cry, then fade away

A VIEW FROM THE CHOIR
[SECTION TWO : PLACES]

The upturned faces of the congregation
Are stained yellow, violet, blue
from the sunlight streaming through
high windows,
portraits of prophets and apostles in vivid purple,
red, orange.

Attentive listeners among the drooping
heads of meditative sleepers
provide unintended canvas for the
hues cast down from
stained glass scenes.

The sun shifts, different well-scrubbed
faces and highlighted
White shirts catch the light and dark
coats absorb it.

Some sit in shadows, while light kisses others.

The message makes no distinction –
amplified equally for the stopped,
ringing and eager ears of all within the cathedral.
Will each sound be heard?
Will words be recognized as sentences?
Will spoken sentences hold meaning?

The sun moves on!
Incandescent illumination lights the nave.

The worship ends.
The sanctuary quiets, gradually
as the last notes of the postlude fade into memory.
Voices greet and take leave in familiar tones.

As the sounds of worship turn to silence,
Sunshine and sermon seem caught
within walls of cold stone and empty benches.

The people depart.
Has the light through prophets stained
their souls?
Will their faces witness the joy of inspiration
and renewal? Can their tongues proclaim
God's majesty?
Will they dare to do His love?

GRAFFITI
[SECTION TWO : PLACES]

Privacy inspires defacement
Limericks engraved on wood, marble, metal
Are these words or drawings?

Outpourings of the quiet concentration
Inspired by intestinal contraction
Or even masturbation??
Alone, yet present in a public place
Sounds of nearby others
Relieving themselves of bodily excretions
Would not seem likely to inspire.

Library restrooms may be candidates
Scratched out instructions for a sexual tryst
Or commentary on current political leadership
Or even on the character of the readership...

Now if the sounds of "other" come with groans
Or if the sound of "others" seems quite strange,
Does the need for commentary provoke?

A line or two of prose or verse?
Or just an exclamation!
Graffiti! Is it more than "breaking wind"?
A passing moment enclosed silence inspires.
Boxed in with just "one's self"
Perhaps just casual comments
On some obscenity of life.

FADING TO BLANK
[SECTION THREE : PUZZLES]

Shades of gray populate the garden furnitured pool room.
With the ever-present TV, I enter –
a voice, an image flickering in the bright sun,
against the shades of gray,
I fade into the flowered wallpaper of nowhere.

She speaks, "I know these strangers. They've come a
long way to see me. What are their names?"

"Oh! The blackness and the cold! Wandering lost
in the dark, Darling! Where are you? Where are you?"

"I've found a haven, by myself, by myself, by myself."

"I've found a haven. Darling! Where are you?"

"No! You say you brought me here."

"Darling! I want to go home!"

"I'm a big girl! Now. I can, will take care of myself."

"Next week. Next week. Next week. I'll go home."

"Progress."

"Did you know I'm going to work again?"

"Yes, I need a job. Typing, a good secretary.
I have good skills. Love! But I can't go home
until we do something about the stairwells."

"Falling down stair wells would be dangerous."

"We don't have stairwells, you say!"

"You know, sometimes people tell me things
I know aren't true. But I pretend to agree, to
know just to please them."

"How can they know?"

"Can they know?"

"They know---.they know!"

Another speaks,
" Have you got a light, Sir?"

"No! Son, ask the man."

"Have you got a light Sir? "Have you got
a light, sir?"" I have a cigarette…"

She speaks, "Cranberry juice, you say."
"Cranberry juice for old folks. Cranberry
"joooose" for strokes"

Gray shades populate the garden furnitured

pool room. The images flicker on the
ever-present television.

I leave as I came a voice, an image,
black in the bright sun.
Amidst the shades of gray,
I fade into the flowered wallpaper of nowhere...

A BUSHEL OF APPLES
[SECTION THREE : PUZZLES]

I don't know how many years they've come out to the farm.
"Helena, Helena—

The Smiths are here for their Spies. Come out and say hello!"

Must be fifteen, twenty years ago, they started
driving up from Elkhart.

The same every year. Three bushels of Spies
and a bushel of Romes.

"The apples look good this year, Max."

Yes, they look good.
A good year but they've come every year...
 good and bad.
Faithful customers, friends, a man can build on that.

"Here's another box to fill."

Every year the same sturdy, cardboard boxes to
fill with firm, fresh apples.

Roll them in gently, so they won't bruise!

Be sure to give full measure!

"There's a few more for the top to round it off."

Something about a bright ripe apple in your hand,
Especially when you've helped it grow.

The noisy, moist crunch
as your teeth break its flesh
Or when Helena's baking apple pie

The tart shimmering cinnamon scent that
tempts your tongue to taste.

"These spies will make good pies."

How many times have I said that and Harry Smith and Joan chuckled at the rhyme?

Well, time to say good-bye; To take the check or change the bill.

"Thanks Harry. See you next year."

Gosh, Harry's getting gray.

"Good to see you, Joan. Come back again."

Come back again.

A bushel of apples is more than a trip to the country.

STRAWBERRY PICKING
[SECTION THREE : PUZZLES]

A field of strawberries
Lost in that summertime of freedom after college.
A frozen moment suspended-----
before marriage and more study.

Who was I then ?
Watching the all the pickers, bending toward the earth
searching for the berries?
A dirty, khaki-clad migrant father sees the boss' son.
("Hi, boss! A smile for your son--whose supervisin'
What else do bosses' sons do?
Nothin'. ")

Gladys, a neighbor, working in the packing shed,
her different time--caught bound in past musings....
Remembering a small, neighbor boy
Stopping by for cookies ....
"How could he be out of college, now---
And getting married?"

Time runs fast for neighbors watching children.
Time drifts slowly past for migrant workers.

Gladys wonders and my thoughts seem
as far away from these home fields
as the clumping rain clouds.

Their thunder and grayness

bring cool respite from the sun-baked search for berries.

"How many beeries in a box to earn a penny?

And if you have to pull their caps for freezin' How many boxes make a dollar?

Or bread to fill the children

Or a bottle to find a spirit lost in the green mazes, wandering in silent search for berries."

My Mom spoons strawberries on cottage cheese and cautions me, "Son, you can't be picker and boss together."

Perhaps you think of strawberries with shortcake

Of summer parties' fun and cake and ice cream,

Frolicking feet on a carpet of green

A carefree breeze and swinging hair.

Pain plates the berries, I remember,

Tatters for clothes, sun-burned nose

Strained back and aching brain.

Grim reflections dim the supermarket luster.

Reclaim that box of berries

Empty!

Comes the unspoken refrain

"Dim the sun!"

"Cloud the sky!"

"Bring the wind!"

And rain, rain.....

THE NEUTRON BOMB
[SECTION THREE : PUZZLES]

A neutron bomb landed quietly on our campus.
Launched from a high place by the system with
a triggering device designed by administrative forces
a neutron bomb landed on our campus.

One by one students and faculty started falling dead...
on the cool spring green lawns
Dead at a lectern in the classrooms
Dead bent over a microscope in a laboratory
Dead in a the middle of dress rehearsal
Dead hands still on the keyboard
Dead in gymnasium and swimming pool

The campus grew very silent.

People arrived from across the state and even
from outside the country wearing those bulky
suits that protect you from deadly radiation
they came to recover the bodies
of sons, daughters, sisters, brothers, husbands,
wives, uncles, aunts,
Grandmothers, grandfathers. They took the bodies away.

A memorial plaque was placed.

Life hummed busily inside the shielded tower of
administration.... Thirty-foot-thick, ten stories tall slabs

of lead—kept the neutrons out of the nerve
center of campus activity
Kept the news out.
Kept the views out
of a dying learning community.
nevertheless. The lights stayed on. The toilets flushed.
Elevators operated up and down.
Air conditioners cooled and furnaces heated.
even the books in the library were unharmed …

On the day the neutron bomb landed on our campus.

Sometime after the neutron bomb landed on
our campus an inspection tour was held.
A heliocopter carrying
The governor, legislators, trustees and presdient
of the school flew over the scene.

They marveled at the tidines of the place.

They commented on the fine new buildings.
They complimented the inventory of equipment and
Library holdings.
They commended the president on the fact
that no complaints had been received from faculty
or. Students.
A neutron bomb landed on our campus.
it killed all the faculty and students.
is a university more than its facilities?

THE BLINDFOLD
[SECTION THREE : PUZZLES]

Consider the statue of a woman
Clothed in flowing gown
Her outstretched arm holds a balance
A way to compare the weight of two objects.

The woman's face is comely.

Around her head a cloth is tied
Covering both her eyes.
She cannot see the way the balance tips.

I have heard that this statue is
The sculptor's idea to represent the principle
"Justice is blind!"

This is not the voluntary blindness of love!
This blindness is enforced.

Who placed the blindfold on this silent lady?
What does that wretched folded cloth foretell?
Do images deceive more quickly than do words?
Who claims that one picture is worth one thousand words?
Words move slowly as they assault our minds!

Perhaps the weight of arguments can be
observed, when balanced against others.
But images, images, images can they be weighed?

Images are like music—I can feel them.
Images can be described in words,
but some verbal translations remove what certainty
was there before...

I want to say that images create a passion to convict
To make a judgment as to who is right or wrong.
Eyewitnesses testify with certainty.

Radical makeovers and successful disguises
suggest that you should only believe half of what you see!

Should eyewitnesses be required to wear blindfolds too?
Wouldn't that make their testimony more convincing.

Does blindness to the moment symbolize neutrality?

Our world is full of images today.

Our world is full of words that represent.

Our world is full of manufactured faces,
posed and retouched photos—purposeful propaganda.

I cannot tell a lie. My lips are sealed in silent testimony.

TERMITES
[SECTION THREE : PUZZLES]

Termites will eat your house,
They come!
Leave you standing without a home.
There you are!

Naked, alone!
No solid board to call your own.
Abandoned! Abandoned!

A suburban skeleton standing there,
With broken glass, half-eaten chairs,
Tangled draperies, rustling the air,
Neighbors smirking behind their stares.
Scorned! Scorned!

All because you failed to see.
The termites swarming around your trees
Nor paid the exterminator inspection fee
To come and say, "Oh, Mercy me!"
Forgotten! Forgotten!

Such are the times of suburban bliss
When no neighbor cares a bad, damn piss
Unless your house is better than hiss
And your name appears on a better list.
Hated! Hated!

Oh! The termites they come
and the termites they go.
Maybe they'll wait for a year or so
To fill their bellies with another's hole
And the mice they come and the mice they go
Blinded! Blinded!

STRUGGLE
[SECTION THREE : PUZZLES]

A giant stirs from slumber in the South.
Pure words in honeyed voices fail to form.
The children born at Babel stay forlorn.
Pride stalks, the strutter, the dark behemoth.

The silent symbol of a surface world
The quiet, callous calm, these hundred years
Cast singing warriors, whom the lynch mob fears,
Unrecognized, behind black faces blurred.

Old hatreds flicker in the cross-bright flames.
Where are the words that two men spoke as one?
Loud horns cry out, while wealth divides the tongue,
And men call color scores of other names.

Trembling now, we stand in worlds we dreamed
You and Yours in some uncharted world.
Cross and crown, the banners are unfurled.
New earth is born. Amidst the hymns and screams.

I AM
AMERICA WEEPING
[SECTION THREE : PUZZLES]

I feel America fading,
a country once borne strong
out of the womb of revolutionary courage.
The First New Nation—
Free from the heritage of monarchy,
not owing to any particular religious tradition.
Declaring itself under God—
but not requiring allegiance to any well-turned-out theology.

Now a too ripe apple,
America rots in a surfeit of pleasure,
an affluent society
that has lost the edge—
provided by expanding frontiers.

Too much dulls the consciousness.

Moral leadership decays
jaded by old knowledge
and new compromises---
 taken to "close the deal."

I see America falling,
turning inward-only to find an empty heart
beating to an economy tuned to lust,
carnal delights, once suppressed

become the only source of new passion for ... freedom?
Legacy of the sixties,

The word, "free" that sticks in my throat.

For I am America,
and I weep, perhaps,
the last tears of hope.

CALOUSED CONSCIENCES
[SECTION THREE : PUZZLES]

Remember America agonized,
like some gigantic Lincoln.
Bent with sun-browned face lined with concern
pursuing justice,
striding slowly forward through winds of change.

No! Not that vision.

America—a stone cold monument
A failed republic, long ago frozen.
Hard and unrelenting
Cracking, instead of yielding
To pain, poverty, pressure of protest and…

How easily we think about the multitude
experiencing poverty or pain.

Our news magazines and papers report injuries to the poor.
Immigrants choosing to leave rather than be deported.
Next to advertisements for vacations in Jamaica and luxury cars
Consecutive pages in our reading material--
Stories of environmental degradation lay open
On beautifully crafted tables
In our upholstery insulated "living rooms".

An easily overlooked aspect
Of the electronic miracles of television, internet, radio access

to information bringing humans close — into a worldwide tribe
The well-cushioned coffin of the easy chair dims our vision.

Closeness in this context breeds the callousness
Of too easily won familiarity
No pain born of black, brown or red skin
No blood, no empty stomach fighting an illness,

you can't afford more than a brief glimpse
through an electronic window at lives beyond the
barrier of leisure..

An experience, a late movie—perhaps, a half-waking dream.
A little like reading the impassioned commentary by radicals,
who would rather rant than act?

I have seen your documentaries America.
Financed by companies who'd rather reveal the problems
They created than work to solve them-–-
and thus through an implicit, contrite confession
purge themselves of guilt...
Listening to the chorus of our voices chanting.

"Oh! How awful!" "Oh! How true!"
Beating on our breasts and doing nothing..

God.

I wonder what a nation of white-washed tombs would look like?
White-washed tombs instead of people ...
I guess there wouldn't be eyes to see.

Or ears to hear the poison wind
whispering among the tombs.
"Oh! How awful!"

"Oh! How true!"

YOUNG AT HEART
[SECTION THREE : PUZZLES]

As my Father grew older he had several
favorite songs.

One was from the movie version of the
Mary Poppins stories. "Let's go fly a kite…"

I remember times when I was very young that we
flew Or tried to fly a kite together.

No fancy kite, but one with a tail made of cloth and rags.

And it was my Father who taught me to play
"knife baseball" with a jack knife and a piece of old lumber.
My uncles were the ones who took me fishing.
But my Father was our club's 4-H Leader in charge.

Perhaps his favorite song,
was one recorded by the venerable Jimmy Durante.
In his raspy voice He sang…
"Don't you know that it's worth
Every treasure on earth
To be Young at Heart…"

Clearly- a man who simply enjoyed gazing
At the golden glow of a ripe peach in his hand,
Reflecting the rays of sunset—
Was young at heart…

His heart was that of a poet,
And a song was often in his head,
if not on his lips...

Like Will Rogers, one of his heroes,
he never met a man He didn't like.

He loved life,
but did not fear death
He told me not long before he died in his sleep...
That he thought he had finished writing his memoir...

He was truly and forever will be young at heart,
Even in eternity..... Wherever that exists.

ANGEL TONGUES
[SECTION THREE : PUZZLES]

I think that I shall never dream
Beyond the worlds conceived by man.
I think that I shall never know
What made the stars begin to glow,
Or grasp the secret mystery
That lies within infinity.

I think that I shall never hear
A sound as silent as the night.
I think that I shall never see
A word born in a language free,
Or chart a bee's returning line---
From flower to hive in record time.

I think that I shall never love
People as much as God loves me.
I think that I shall never hate
Person whose need determines fate,
Despise a pauper's outstretched hand
Fail to share my blessings grand.

I think that I shall never taste
The water found in springs on Mars.
I think that I shall never feel
The roughness of a mammoth's tail
Or sandpaper seqoyah bark
In some Tasmanian National Park.

Perhaps when tragedy becomes
The comedy I see in life,
Then men will speak with angel tongues
And laughter put an end to strife.

THE LAST WORD
[SECTION THREE : PUZZLES]

The image is fine.

A metaphor marvelous! A simile analogous,

suggesting the real... But what could be better

than breaking words' fetters

and knowing in thoughts that we feel.

www.ingramcontent.com/pod-product-compliance
Lightning Source LLC
LaVergne TN
LVHW041636070526
838199LV00052B/3391